Good Seasons

Casual ENTERTAINING

*A*re casual get-togethers becoming all too rare because of busy schedules? Then this book is for you. The GOOD SEASONS® Kitchens bring you great ideas for meals that come together quickly and spontaneously.

Best yet, the recipes in this book feature versatile, top-quality products that make foods fresh-tasting and easy to prepare. You'll see how GOOD SEASONS® Salad Dressing Mixes, COLAVITA® Extra Virgin Olive Oil and Red Wine Vinegar, ATHENOS® Feta Cheese, DI GIORNO® Parmesan Cheese and HEINZ® Apple Cider Vinegar open up opportunities for entertaining any night of the week, with as much ease as today's hectic lifestyles demand. You'll impress your guests with the flavors in these festive entrées, side dishes and summer salads.

 Illustrations with each recipe indicate whether you need an envelope of GOOD SEASONS Salad Dressing Mix (shown top left) or prepared dressing (cruet, shown lower left). Also, preparation and cooking times are given to help you plan your time.

So enjoy the simplicity and great flavors that *Casual Entertaining* and these featured products bring to your table. You'll see how easy it is to make this season, and every season, a good season.

PICTURED ON THE COVER: Caribbean Jerk Chicken (see recipe, page 10) and Black Bean and Mango Salsa (see recipe, page 32).

Casual
ENTERTAINING

© Copyright Kraft Foods, Inc. and Meredith Corporation, 1998. All rights reserved. Canadian BN 12348 2887 RT. Printed in Hong Kong. The Better Your Home Series® is published by Meredith Custom Publishing, Publishing Group of Meredith Corporation, 1716 Locust St., Des Moines, IA 50309-3023.

GOOD SEASONS, ATHENOS and DI GIORNO are registered trademarks of Kraft Foods, Inc. COLAVITA is a registered trademark of Oleifici Colavita S.p.A. HEINZ is a registered trademark of H. J. Heinz Co.

Easy

Although the word "entertaining" may conjure up images of hours spent in the kitchen, it doesn't have to be that way. Entertaining can be as unassuming as inviting the neighbors over to kick off the weekend or to open the deck for the summer.

GOOD SEASONS *Casual Entertaining* is all about making it easy on yourself so that your guests—and you—can enjoy each other around good food. Here are a few tips to simplify any gathering:

- When choosing the menu, plan either all finger foods or go with sit-down foods that require cutlery (it's easier to serve just one style).
- Begin with fresh, high-quality, flavorful ingredients. For example, GOOD SEASONS Salad Dressing Mixes are sure to bring

success to any meal because you make the dressing fresh yourself.

- Look to the produce aisle or salad bar of your supermarket for precut vegetables and ready-to-eat fruit. Then, artfully arrange them on pretty platters and serve with dips.
  - Seek out a reliable European-style bakery as a source of good bread. Served with Seasoned Spread on page 19 or used in Bruschetta on page 88, outstanding bread can become speedy appetizers as well as complementing the main course.
- For dessert, consider a favorite high-quality ice cream or sorbet from your supermarket, or tap into local restaurants or bakeries that specialize in pies, cakes, tarts and pastries. That way, all you have to do is brew coffee.

- Rely on fresh, simple, reliable recipes, such as the ones in this book from the GOOD SEASONS Kitchens. An illustration with each recipe indicates whether you need to start with an envelope of GOOD SEASONS Salad Dressing Mix (see illustration of package at left) or prepared dressing (see illustration of cruet at left).

START WITH A GREAT BLEND OF FLAVORS

GOOD SEASONS Salad Dressing Mixes do more than deliciously dress a salad—they're handy seasoning blends that let you add distinctive flavor to all types of foods without measuring numerous ingredients.

To use as a salad dressing, prepare according to the directions on any GOOD SEASONS product or the cruet kit (as shown above) or enjoy creative control by varying the type or amount of vinegar and oil to suit your taste. It's easy and it only takes a few minutes to make. See the sidebar on page 7 for suggestions, then experiment with any of the GOOD SEASONS Salad Dressing Mix flavors.

MIX IT FRESH IN YOUR CRUET

The GOOD SEASONS® cruet is not only attractive but convenient for both mixing and serving. To prepare dressing for salads or for one of the recipes in this book, simply add the ingredients to the lines on the cruet as follows:

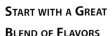

Pour vinegar to –V– line (1/4 cup). For an all-purpose dressing with a fruity flavor, use HEINZ® Apple Cider Vinegar.

Add water to the –W– line (3 Tbsp.). Add contents of the envelope; shake vigorously until well blended.

Pour oil to –O– line (1/2 cup). For a rich Italian flavor, try COLAVITA® Extra Virgin Olive Oil. Shake again until well blended. To maintain freshness, refrigerate up to 4 weeks.

THE INCREDIBLE VARIETY AND VERSATILITY OF

GOOD SEASONS

SALAD DRESSING MIXES GIVE CREATIVE COOKS A JUMP-START IN PREPARING FRESH, FULL-FLAVORED FOODS.

GOOD SEASONS Salad Dressing Mixes are all natural with no preservatives. This makes them a natural choice for entertaining and everyday meals, when you want to create impressive fare with ease. Of course, GOOD SEASONS Salad Dressing Mixes are always a fresh way to toss a salad, because you make the dressing yourself with ingredients on hand.

ADD RED WINE VINEGAR AND OLIVE OIL

An essential element of a good dressing is a fine vinegar. With its tart and fruity essence, COLAVITA Red Wine Vinegar makes a good, all purpose choice.

In addition to the seasonings and the vinegar, the third and vital element of a good dressing is the oil. Olive oil, such as COLAVITA Extra Virgin Olive Oil, is the versatile oil for cooking or as a condiment, whether the dish you're preparing is American, Italian, Mediterranean or from another international cooking style.

Use COLAVITA Extra Virgin Olive Oil to prepare any of the GOOD SEASONS Salad Dressing Mixes for a richer flavor. The resulting dressing also makes a terrific dip for crusty bread or savory sauce to brush on when grilling meats, fish, poultry and vegetables.

When choosing olive oil, choose extra virgin olive oil. Unlike other cooking oils, extra virgin olive oil is not chemically extracted or refined. What's more, olive oil contains no cholesterol and less saturated fat than butter.

ROUND OUT THE MENU WITH CHEESE

Cheeses, like olive oils, have regional distinctions—and they also have a myriad of uses. A good, high-quality, sharp cheese such as feta—a white, semisoft, crumbly cheese— adds loads of flavor to all kinds of recipes. Easy-to-use ATHENOS Feta Cheeses are often crumbled in salads as well as used in cooking.

Whether you're enjoying traditional feta cheese or one of the flavored varieties, you'll discover the distinctive flavor of feta adds a special note to the overall dish.

With its delightfully nutty flavor, Parmesan cheese is another versatile, sharp cheese. DI GIORNO Grated Parmesan Cheese is used for blending into creamy risottos, lasagna and spreads. DI GIORNO Shredded Parmesan Cheese shines as a topping for pizza and as a garnish atop salads.

ADD VARIETY TO DISHES WITH VINEGAR

Just as cheeses have distinctive flavors, so do vinegars. One of the most popular vinegars—HEINZ Apple Cider Vinegar—has a fruity flavor that is wonderful when combined with any GOOD SEASONS Salad Dressing Mix flavor. This all-natural ingredient contains no additives or preservatives and is made only from sun-ripened corn, juicy apples and the finest wine. Its pure flavor helps to heighten and bring out the fresh taste of summer salads and vegetables. When your food is at its best, you are, too.

EXPANDING YOUR FLAVOR OPTIONS

For more flavor choices, experiment with oil and vinegar combinations as you prepare GOOD SEASONS Salad Dressing Mixes. Below are a few suggestions:

- For a richer Italian flavor, use $\frac{1}{2}$ cup COLAVITA Extra Virgin Olive Oil when preparing GOOD SEASONS Cheese Garlic, Roasted Garlic or Gourmet Parmesan Italian Salad Dressing Mixes.

- Lend a robust tomato flavor to GOOD SEASONS Honey French Salad Dressing Mix by using tomato juice or spicy seasoned tomato juice instead of water.

- Personalize the flavor of your GOOD SEASONS Cheese Garlic Salad Dressing Mix by using herb-infused oils such as garlic, tarragon or basil oils.

- For a simple flavor zip, try a fruit-flavored vinegar such as raspberry or mango when preparing GOOD SEASONS Mild Italian Salad Dressing Mix.

- Enrich the flavor of GOOD SEASONS Fat Free Italian Salad Dressing Mix by substituting orange, cranberry or grapefruit juice for the water.

The Allure of the Grill

THERE'S JUST SOMETHING SPECIAL ABOUT GRILLING.
IT'S SIMPLE. IT FILLS THE AIR WITH TANTALIZING
AROMAS. AND, BEST OF ALL, IT INFUSES ANY FOOD
THAT THE SMOKE AND FIRE TOUCHES WITH THE
DISTINCTIVE FLAVOR OF THE OUTDOORS.

Caribbean Jerk Chicken SEE RECIPE, PAGE 10

Caribbean Jerk

CHICKEN

GRILLING GIVES THIS ISLAND-STYLE CHICKEN GREAT SMOKY FLAVOR. PICTURED ON PAGES 8–9 AND ON THE COVER.

- **1 envelope GOOD SEASONS Italian Salad Dressing Mix**
- **2 Tbsp.** *each* **brown sugar, oil and soy sauce**
- **1 tsp.** *each* **ground cinnamon and thyme**
- **¹/₂ tsp. ground red pepper**
- **2¹/₂ lb. chicken pieces**

MIX all ingredients except chicken in small bowl until well blended.

POUR dressing over chicken; cover. Refrigerate 1 hour to marinate. Drain; discard dressing mixture.

PLACE on greased grill over hot coals or on rack of broiler pan 5 to 7 inches from heat. Grill or broil 40 to 45 minutes or until cooked through, turning frequently. Makes 6 to 8 servings.

PREP TIME: 10 MINUTES PLUS MARINATING
GRILLING OR BROILING TIME: 45 MINUTES

Sassy Southern

CHICKEN

A TOUCH OF WHISKEY AND HONEY FRENCH SALAD DRESSING GIVE THIS CHICKEN DISH A SOUTHERN ACCENT.

- **3 Tbsp.** *each* **HEINZ Apple Cider Vinegar and whiskey**

- **1 envelope GOOD SEASONS Honey French Salad Dressing Mix**
- **¹/₂ cup oil**
- **1 lb. boneless skinless chicken breast halves**

MIX all ingredients except chicken in small bowl until well blended.

POUR dressing mixture over chicken; cover. Refrigerate 1 hour to marinate. Drain; discard dressing mixture.

PLACE chicken on greased grill over hot coals. Grill 15 to 20 minutes or until chicken is cooked through. Makes 4 servings.

PREP TIME: 10 MINUTES PLUS MARINATING
GRILLING TIME: 20 MINUTES

GRILLED CHICKEN
Salad

CRISP AND FLAVORFUL, THIS MAIN-DISH
SALAD IS A WELCOME SIGHT ON ANY
SUMMERTIME TABLE.

 1 envelope GOOD SEASONS Gourmet
Caesar Salad Dressing Mix
1/4 cup lemon juice
4 boneless skinless chicken breast
halves
6 cups torn romaine lettuce
1 cup croutons
1/2 cup (2 oz.) DI GIORNO Grated
Parmesan Cheese

PREPARE salad dressing mix as directed
on envelope, except substituting juice
or vinegar. Reserve 1/2 cup of the
dressing mixture.

POUR remaining dressing over chicken; cover.
Refrigerate 1 hour to marinate. Drain;
discard dressing.

PLACE chicken on greased grill over hot coals
or on rack of broiler pan 3 to 5 inches from
heat. Grill or broil 10 minutes on each side
or until chicken is cooked through. Cut
into slices.

TOSS lettuce, croutons and cheese with
reserved 1/2 cup dressing. Arrange chicken
slices over salad. Makes 4 servings.

PREP TIME: 15 MINUTES PLUS MARINATING
GRILLING OR BROILING TIME:
   20 MINUTES

HEINZ WHITE AND APPLE CIDER VINEGARS CAN HELP KEEP GREENS

AND OTHER VEGETABLES AT THEIR PEAK. TO CLEAN GREENS, VEGETABLES

CRISP, CLEAN
AND FRUITS, WASH THEM WITH A MIXTURE OF 2 TO

GREENS
3 TABLESPOONS OF HEINZ VINEGAR PER QUART OF

WATER. TO REVIVE WILTED GREENS, SOAK THEM IN A

QUART OF COLD WATER AND 1 TABLESPOON OF

HEINZ VINEGAR.

Margarita Shrimp

AND VEGETABLE KABOBS

REMINISCENT OF THEIR FESTIVE NAMESAKE, THESE TEQUILA- AND LIME-INFUSED KABOBS WOULD BE JUST RIGHT WITH FRESH TORTILLAS. WARM THE TORTILLAS IN A FOIL PACK ON THE EDGE OF THE GRILL WHILE THE KABOBS ARE COOKING.

1/4 **cup *each* tequila and lime juice**
1 **envelope GOOD SEASONS Italian *or* Zesty Italian Salad Dressing Mix**
1/2 **cup oil**
1 **lb. medium shrimp, cleaned***
Assorted cut-up fresh vegetables (red peppers, onions, zucchini, yellow summer squash, mushrooms)

MIX tequila, juice, salad dressing mix and oil in cruet or small bowl as directed on envelope. Pour over shrimp and vegetables; cover. Refrigerate 1 hour to marinate. Drain; discard dressing.

ARRANGE shrimp and vegetables on skewers.

PLACE kabobs on greased grill over hot coals. Grill 10 to 15 minutes or until shrimp turn pink and vegetables are tender-crisp, turning once. Serve with rice, if desired. Makes 4 servings.

*NOTE: For an extra-special presentation, leave the tails on the shrimp.

PREP TIME: 20 MINUTES
    PLUS MARINATING
GRILLING TIME: 15 MINUTES

GRILLED

Italian

BALSAMIC VINEGAR, USED IN THIS ARRANGED SALAD, GETS ITS RICH, SWEET TASTE FROM YEARS OF AGING IN WOODEN BARRELS.

- **1 envelope GOOD SEASONS Italian Salad Dressing Mix**
- **$^1/_3$ cup COLAVITA Extra Virgin Olive Oil**
- **$^1/_4$ cup COLAVITA Balsamic Vinegar**
- **1 lb. medium shrimp, cleaned**
- **$^1/_2$ lb. hard salami, cut into $^1/_4$-inch cubes**
- **$^1/_2$ lb. fresh mozzarella cheese, thinly sliced**
- **2 Tbsp. chopped fresh basil**

MIX salad dressing mix, oil and vinegar in cruet or small bowl as directed on envelope.

THREAD shrimp and salami onto four skewers.

PLACE kabobs on greased grill over medium-hot coals. Grill 3 to 4 minutes on each side or until shrimp turn pink. Remove from skewers.

ARRANGE cheese slices on platter; top with shrimp and salami. Drizzle with dressing mixture; sprinkle with basil. Serve with bread, if desired. Makes 12 servings.

PREP TIME: 10 MINUTES
GRILLING TIME: 8 MINUTES

MIX UP YOUR FAVORITE **GOOD SEASONS** SALAD DRESSING MIX AND KEEP

SALAD DRESSING
SOME ON HAND TO ADD A FLAVOR BOOST TO ALL TYPES OF FOODS. (IT WILL

TO THE RESCUE
STORE IN THE REFRIGERATOR FOR UP TO 4 WEEKS.) USE IT AS A DIP FOR

CRUSTY BREAD OR VEGETABLES. BRUSH SOME ON MEATS,

SEAFOOD OR CHICKEN BEFORE GRILLING OR ROASTING. SAUTÉ

VEGETABLES OR MEATS IN THE DRESSING FOR EXTRA ZING.

L E M O N

Dill Fish

MEATY SALMON OR SWORDFISH
MAKES A PERFECT MATCH FOR THE ASSERTIVE
FLAVORS IN THIS ZESTY MARINADE. SERVE
THE ENTRÉE ALONGSIDE PASTA OR RICE.

- **1 envelope GOOD SEASONS Zesty Italian *or* Italian Salad Dressing Mix**
- **¹/₄ cup oil**
- **¹/₄ cup chopped fresh parsley**
- **2 Tbsp. lemon juice**
- **1 tsp. dill weed**
- **2 lb. salmon fillets *or* swordfish steaks**

MIX salad dressing mix, oil, parsley, juice and dill in cruet or small bowl as directed on envelope.

RUB over fish in large baking dish; cover. Refrigerate 1 hour to marinate. Drain; discard marinade.

PLACE fish on greased grill over hot coals or on rack of broiler pan 2 to 4 inches from heat. Grill or broil 4 to 5 minutes on each side or until fish flakes easily with fork. Makes 6 to 8 servings.

PREP TIME: 10 MINUTES PLUS MARINATING
GRILLING OR BROILING TIME: 10 MINUTES

FRESHLY SQUEEZED LEMON JUICE GIVES A TANTALIZING CITRUS FLAVOR TO ALL

LEMON JUICE
SAVVY

TYPES OF DISHES. TO GET THE MOST JUICE, PURCHASE A LEMON

THAT IS HEAVY FOR ITS SIZE. BEFORE SQUEEZING, LEAVE THE

LEMON AT ROOM TEMPERATURE FOR 30 MINUTES. THEN

ROLL IT UNDER THE PALM OF YOUR HAND A FEW TIMES SO MORE

JUICE WILL FLOW. A MEDIUM LEMON WILL YIELD ABOUT 3 TABLESPOONS JUICE.

Steak &

ONE IS JUICY AND SUBSTANTIAL, THE OTHER CRISP, GREEN AND LIGHT—STEAK AND SPINACH ARE A NATURAL COMBINATION. SERVE THIS WHOLE-MEAL SALAD WITH CRUSTY FRENCH BREAD.

- **1 envelope GOOD SEASONS Gourmet Parmesan Italian Salad Dressing Mix**
- **$^1/_3$ cup HEINZ Apple Cider Vinegar**
- **$^1/_3$ cup COLAVITA Extra Virgin Olive Oil**
- **1 clove garlic, minced**
- **1 beef sirloin steak, $^1/_2$ to $^3/_4$ inch thick (1 lb.)**
- **8 cups torn spinach**
- **1 cup sliced mushrooms**
- **1 large tomato, cut into wedges**
- **$^1/_4$ cup sliced green onions**

MIX salad dressing mix, vinegar, olive oil and garlic in cruet or small bowl as directed on envelope. Reserve $^1/_3$ cup of the dressing mixture; refrigerate.

POUR remaining dressing over steak; cover. Refrigerate 1 hour to marinate. Drain; discard dressing mixture.

PLACE steak on greased grill over hot coals or on rack of broiler pan 2 to 3 inches from heat. Grill or broil 10 minutes on each side or to desired doneness. Cut into slices.

TOSS spinach, mushrooms, tomato and onions with reserved $^1/_3$ cup dressing mixture. Arrange steak slices over salad. Makes 4 servings.

CHICKEN & SPINACH SALAD: Substitute 1 lb. boneless skinless chicken breasts for steak.

PREP TIME: 10 MINUTES PLUS MARINATING
GRILLING OR BROILING TIME: 20 MINUTES

Zesty Burgers

THESE SAVORY BURGERS ARE UNBEATABLE. SET OUT AN ASSORTMENT OF FIXINGS— LETTUCE, TOMATO, ONION, PICKLES, CHEESES, HOT PEPPERS, ETC.—AND LET GUESTS BUILD THEIR OWN MASTERPIECES.

1¹/₂ **lb. ground beef**
1 **envelope GOOD SEASONS Zesty Italian *or* Italian Salad Dressing Mix**

MIX meat and salad dressing mix. Shape into 4 patties.

PLACE patties on greased grill over hot coals. Grill 6 to 7 minutes on each side or to desired doneness. Makes 4.

PREP TIME: 5 MINUTES
GRILLING TIME: 14 MINUTES

SPICY GRILLED Mushrooms

TRY STEAK AND MUSHROOMS WITH A TWIST! COOK YOUR FAVORITE CUT OF BEEF ON THE GRILL AND SERVE IT WITH THESE ASIAN-SPICED MUSHROOMS.

¹/₄ **cup HEINZ Apple Cider Vinegar**
3 **Tbsp. soy sauce**
1 **envelope GOOD SEASONS Oriental Sesame Salad Dressing Mix**
¹/₂ **cup oil**
1 **to 2 tsp. hot pepper sauce**
2 **cloves garlic, minced**
1 **lb. fresh shiitake *or* button mushrooms, stems removed**

MIX vinegar, soy sauce, salad dressing mix, oil, hot pepper sauce and garlic in cruet or small bowl as directed on envelope. Pour over mushrooms in large bowl. Let stand 30 minutes to marinate. Drain, reserving dressing mixture.

PLACE mushrooms on greased grill over medium coals or on rack of broiler pan 3 to 5 inches from heat. Grill or broil mushrooms 3 to 5 minutes on each side or until tender and slightly crisp, turning and brushing frequently with reserved dressing mixture. Makes 4 to 6 servings.

PREP TIME: 5 MINUTES PLUS MARINATING
GRILLING OR BROILING TIME: 10 MINUTES

Seasoned

THE USES FOR THIS DELICIOUS SPREAD ARE NEARLY LIMITLESS. IN ADDITION TO GRILLED CORN OR BREAD, TRY IT ON GRILLED FISH OR SEAFOOD, BAKED POTATOES, PASTA, RICE AND STEAMED OR GRILLED VEGETABLES.

1 envelope GOOD SEASONS Italian Salad Dressing Mix
$^1/_2$ cup (1 stick) butter *or* margarine, softened

MIX salad dressing mix and butter until well blended.

SERVE on corn, hot cooked vegetables or pasta. Makes $^1/_2$ cup.

PREP TIME: 5 MINUTES

GRILLED CORN: Pull back husks from ears of corn; remove silks. Replace husks. Soak in water for 1 hour. Place in husks on greased grill over medium coals. Grill 20 minutes or until tender. Remove husks and generously brush corn with Seasoned Spread.

GRILLED BREAD: Spread both sides of thick crusted Italian bread, flour tortillas, hamburger buns or pita bread with Seasoned Spread. Place on greased grill over medium coals. Grill 2 minutes or until lightly toasted. (Serve grilled hamburger buns with Zesty Burgers— see recipe, page 18.)

GRILLED

Italian Focaccia

Bake bread on the grill? You bet!
High heat gives this Italian
flatbread a super-crisp crust.

- 1 **pkg. (16 oz.) hot roll mix**
- 1 **envelope GOOD SEASONS Italian Salad Dressing Mix**
- 3 **Tbsp. COLAVITA Extra Virgin Olive Oil, divided**
- 1 **cup DI GIORNO Shredded Parmesan Cheese**
- 2 **plum tomatoes, sliced**
- 2 **Tbsp. fresh basil leaves**

Mix hot roll mix, yeast packet and salad dressing mix. Add 1¼ cups hot water (120°F to 130°F) and 2 tablespoons of the oil. Stir until soft dough forms and dough pulls away from side of bowl.

Knead dough on lightly floured surface about 5 minutes or until smooth and elastic. Shape dough into 2 (10-inch) rounds. Cover with plastic wrap or towel. Let rise in warm place 15 minutes.

Place dough rounds on greased grill over medium-low coals. Grill 4 minutes; turn. Brush with remaining 1 tablespoon oil. Top with cheese, tomatoes and basil. Grill an additional 4 minutes or until bottom crust is golden brown. Makes 2 bread rounds or 16 servings.

Prep Time: 10 minutes plus rising
Grilling Time: 8 minutes

POTATO SALAD

With just the right tang from HEINZ Vinegar, this potato salad is the perfect side to a main event of grilled pork chops or bratwurst.

1/2 **cup HEINZ Apple Cider Vinegar**
1 **envelope GOOD SEASONS Gourmet Caesar Salad Dressing Mix**
1/4 **cup oil**
6 **medium potatoes, peeled, sliced**
1 **medium onion, chopped**
8 **slices bacon, cut into 1-inch pieces, cooked, crumbled**

Mix vinegar, salad dressing mix and oil in cruet or small bowl as directed on envelope. Toss with vegetables and cooked bacon.

Spoon mixture evenly onto double layer of heavy-duty aluminum foil; close foil to form tightly-sealed pouch.

Place pouch on greased grill over medium coals. Grill 30 minutes, turning and shaking pouch halfway through grilling time. Makes 6 servings.

Prep Time: 15 minutes
Grilling Time: 30 minutes

With foil-packet recipes, such as Hot German Potato Salad, above,

Dinner

cooking a meal on the grill is easy. Simply grill the packet alongside

from the Grill

steaks, chops, burgers, chicken pieces or fish. If the meat or

fish takes longer to cook than the salad, start the meat

first; then, add the packet. After grilling, open the foil

slowly, being careful to allow steam to escape away from you.

Caesar
P O T A T O E S

These roasted potatoes with a confetti of peppers and onions have all the great flavors of their namesake salad—lemon, garlic, black pepper and tangy Parmesan cheese.

 1 envelope GOOD SEASONS Gourmet Caesar *or* Italian Salad Dressing Mix
$^1/_4$ cup *each* HEINZ Apple Cider Vinegar and oil
$1^1/_2$ lb. red potatoes, cut into chunks
1 medium red *or* green pepper, cut into 1-inch pieces
1 medium onion, cut into 1-inch pieces

PREPARE salad dressing mix in cruet or small bowl as directed on envelope with vinegar and oil, omitting water.

TOSS remaining ingredients with dressing mixture. Spoon evenly onto double layer of heavy-duty aluminum foil; close foil to form tightly-sealed pouch.

PLACE pouch on greased grill over medium coals. Grill 30 to 35 minutes or until potatoes are tender, turning and shaking halfway through grilling time. Makes 4 to 6 servings.

GREAT IN THE OVEN, TOO! Prepare as directed except for grilling. Spoon evenly into 15x10x1-inch baking pan lined with foil. Bake at 400°F for 40 minutes or until potatoes are tender.

PREP TIME: 10 MINUTES
GRILLING TIME: 35 MINUTES
    OR
BAKING TIME: 40 MINUTES

Salad

This colorful salad is just as good with burgers and frankfurters as it is with chops and steaks.

1/4 **cup HEINZ Apple Cider Vinegar**
2 **Tbsp. water**
1 **envelope GOOD SEASONS Gourmet Parmesan Italian *or* Italian Salad Dressing Mix**
1/3 **cup COLAVITA Extra Virgin Olive Oil**
1 **lb. small red potatoes, cut into quarters**
1 ***each* zucchini and yellow squash, halved lengthwise, cut into 1/2-inch chunks**
1 **cup slivered red onion**

Mix vinegar, water, salad dressing mix and oil in cruet or small bowl as directed on envelope. Toss with vegetables.

Spoon mixture evenly onto double layer of heavy-duty aluminum foil; close foil to form tightly sealed pouch.

Place pouch on greased grill over medium coals. Grill 30 minutes, turning and shaking pouch halfway through grilling time. Garnish with fresh rosemary, if desired. Makes 6 servings.

Cook on the Range, Too! Prepare dressing as directed; set aside. Boil potatoes in 6 quarts water for 10 minutes. Add zucchini, squash and onion; boil 5 minutes or until vegetables are tender. Drain; toss with dressing. Serve immediately.

Prep Time: 10 minutes
Grilling Time: 30 minutes
    or
Cooking Time: 15 minutes

DIRECT GRILLING

Place the meat, poultry or fish on the greased rack of an uncovered grill directly over the preheated coals. Grill the meat, poultry or fish for the time given below or until done, turning halfway through the grilling time.

Cut	Thickness/ Weight	Coal Temperature	Doneness	Direct-Grilling Time
Ground meat patties	³/₄ inch (4 per lb.)	Medium	No pink remains	14 to 18 minutes
Beef steak (porterhouse, rib, rib eye, sirloin, T-bone, tenderloin, top loin)	1 inch 1¹/₄ to 1¹/₂ inches	Medium Medium	Medium rare Medium Medium rare Medium	8 to 12 minutes 12 to 15 minutes 14 to 18 minutes 18 to 22 minutes
Beef flank steak	³/₄ to 1 inch	Medium	Medium	12 to 14 minutes
Pork chop	³/₄ inch 1¹/₄ to 1¹/₂ inches	Medium Medium	Medium Medium	8 to 11 minutes 25 to 30 minutes
Frankfurters, smoked bratwurst (fully cooked)	5 to 6 per lb.	Medium-hot	Heated through	3 to 5 minutes
Kabobs (meat)	1-inch cubes	Medium	Medium	12 to 14 minutes
Chicken quarters	2¹/₂ to 3 lb. total	Medium	Tender; cooked through	40 to 50 minutes
Chicken pieces, meaty	2 to 2¹/₂ lb total.	Medium	Tender; cooked through	35 to 45 minutes
Chicken breast half, skinned, boned	4 to 5 oz. each	Medium	Tender; cooked through	12 to 15 minutes
Turkey breast tenderloin steak	4 to 6 oz. each	Medium	Tender; cooked through	12 to 15 minutes
Fish, dressed	¹/₂ to 1¹/₂ lb.	Medium	Flakes	7 to 9 minutes per ¹/₂ lb.
Fish fillets, steaks, cubes (on kabobs)	¹/₂ to 1 inch thick	Medium	Flakes	4 to 6 minutes per ¹/₂-inch thickness
Lobster tails	8 oz.	Medium	Opaque	12 to 15 minutes
Sea scallops (on kabobs)	12 to 15 per lb	Medium	Opaque	5 to 8 minutes
Shrimp (on kabobs)	Medium (20 per lb.) Jumbo (12 to 15 per lb.)	Medium Medium	Opaque Opaque	6 to 8 minutes 10 to 12 minutes

INDIRECT GRILLING

In a grill with a cover, arrange medium-hot coals around a drip pan, then test for medium heat above pan (unless chart says otherwise). Place meat (fat side up), poultry or fish on greased grill rack directly over drip pan, not over coals. Cover; grill for time given or until desired doneness is reached, adding briquettes to maintain heat.

Cut	Thickness/ Weight	Coal Temperature	Doneness	Indirect-Grilling Time
Beef boneless rolled rump roast	4 to 6 lb.	Medium-slow	150° to 160°F	1¼ to 2½ hours
Beef boneless sirloin roast	4 to 6 lb.	Medium-slow	145°F (medium rare) 160°F (medium)	1¾ to 2¼ hours 2¼ to 2¾ hours
Beef eye round roast	2 to 3 lb.	Medium-slow	145°F (medium rare) 160°F (medium)	1 to 1½ hours 1½ to 2 hours
Beef rib eye roast	4 to 6 lb.	Medium-slow	145°F (medium rare) 160°F (medium)	1 to 1½ hours 1½ to 2 hours
Beef rib roast	4 to 6 lb.	Medium-slow	145°F (medium rare) 160°F (medium)	2¼ to 2¾ hours 2¾ to 3¼ hours
Beef round tip roast	3 to 5 lb. 6 to 8 lb.	Medium-slow Medium-slow	145° to 160°F 145° to 160°F	1¼ to 2½ hours 2 to 3¼ hours
Pork boneless top loin roast	2 to 4 lb. (single loin) 3 to 5 lb. (double loin, tied)	Medium-slow Medium-slow	160°F 160°F	1 to 1¼ hours 1¼ to 2¼ hours
Pork ribs, country-style	2 to 4 lb.	Medium	Well-done	1½ to 2 hours
Pork ribs, loin-back, spareribs	2 to 4 lb.	Medium	Well-done	1¼ to 1½ hours
Chicken, broiler-fryer half	1¼ to 1½ lb.	Medium	Tender; cooked through	1 to 1¼ hours
Chicken, whole	2½ to 3 lb. 3½ to 4 lb. 4½ to 5 lb.	Medium Medium Medium	Tender; cooked through	1 to 1¼ hours 1¼ to 1¾ hours 1¾ to 2 hours
Chicken quarters	2½ to 3 lb. total	Medium	Tender; cooked through	50 to 60 minutes
Turkey (do not stuff)	6 to 8 lb. 8 to 12 lb. 12 to 16 lb.	Medium Medium Medium	Tender; cooked through	1¾ to 2¼ hours 2½ to 3½ hours 3 to 4 hours
Turkey breast, whole	4 to 6 lb. 6 to 8 lb.	Medium Medium	Tender; cooked through	1¾ to 2¼ hours 2½ to 3½ hours
Fish, dressed	½ to 1½ lb.	Medium	Flakes	20 to 25 min. per ½ lb.

WITH PORTABLE TREATS, YOU CAN TURN ANY PLACE INTO THE SCENE OF A PARTY. **H**ERE'S A PICNIC BASKETFUL OF EASY-TO-MAKE AND EASY-TO-EAT FOODS THAT TRAVEL WELL TO A PICNIC IN THE PARK, AN OFFICE PARTY OR A LUNCH ON THE SIDELINES OF THE SOCCER FIELD.

Mediterranean Pasta Salad   SEE RECIPE, PAGE 30

Take-Along
Treats

Pasta Salad

Perfect for potluck picnics, this cool and crisp pasta salad studded with crisp zucchini, carrots, sweet pepper, mellow olives and tangy feta cheese makes a lovely accompaniment to grilled chicken. Pictured on pages 28–29.

2¹/₂ **cups (6 oz.) rotini *or* bow tie pasta, cooked, drained**
  1 **each medium zucchini and carrot, thinly sliced**
  1 **each small green and red pepper, chopped**
  1 **can (2¹/₄ oz.) pitted ripe olives, drained**
¹/₂ **cup (2 oz.) ATHENOS Crumbled Feta Cheese**

¹/₂ **tsp. crushed red pepper**
  1 **cup prepared GOOD SEASONS Italian *or* Zesty Italian Salad Dressing**

Mix all ingredients except salad dressing in large bowl. Toss to coat with dressing. Cover.

Refrigerate 1 hour or until ready to serve. Garnish with fresh mint, if desired. Makes 4 to 6 servings.

Prep Time: 20 minutes plus refrigerating

ATHENOS Feta Cheese adds a distinctively Mediterranean flavor to almost any dish. This robust cheese is delicious crumbled over a salad or pasta. Or, simply serve it with olives, bread and wine for a Mediterranean-style summer picnic.

Full-Flavored

Feta Cheese

Italian Dip

PEPPER HALVES MAKE GREAT CONTAINERS
FOR DIPS. THEY'RE COLORFUL, EDIBLE AND
YOU DON'T HAVE TO TAKE THEM HOME.
PICTURED ON PAGE 33.

1 container (16 oz.) sour cream
1 envelope GOOD SEASONS Gourmet
    Parmesan Italian *or* Italian Salad
    Dressing Mix

MIX sour cream and salad dressing mix. Stir in
1 other suggested ingredient, if desired.
Refrigerate. Garnish with cherry tomato
quarters and fresh parsley, if desired. Serve
with crackers, assorted cut-up vegetables or
chips. Makes 2 cups.

SUGGESTED INGREDIENTS:
Stir in any 1 of the following:
  $1/4$ cup sun-dried tomatoes in olive oil,
       drained, chopped
  $1/2$ cup chopped roasted red pepper
  1 tsp. jarred roasted garlic
  1 can ($8^1/2$ oz.) artichoke hearts, drained,
       finely chopped

PREP TIME: 5 MINUTES PLUS
   REFRIGERATING

Snack Mix

BECAUSE IT TRAVELS SO WELL, YOU CAN
ENJOY THIS CRUNCHY SNACK JUST ABOUT
ANYWHERE—THE OFFICE, THE BEACH OR
YOUR PATIO.

6 cups small shredded wheat
    squares cereal
2 cups pretzels
1 cup prepared GOOD SEASONS
    Italian Salad Dressing
$1/2$ cup (2 oz.) DI GIORNO Grated
    Parmesan Cheese
2 cups popped popcorn

PLACE cereal and pretzels in large
bowl. Pour dressing and cheese over
mixture; toss to coat. Spread in
15x10x1-inch baking pan.

BAKE at 300°F for 40 to 45 minutes or
until crisp, stirring every 15 minutes.
Stir in popcorn. Makes 10 cups.

PREP TIME: 10 MINUTES
BAKING TIME: 45 MINUTES

BLACK BEAN AND *Salsa*

Versatile and easy to make, this fresh and colorful salsa is great with tortilla chips or grilled chicken. The addition of quick-cooking brown rice turns it into a light and delicious main-dish salad. Also pictured on the cover.

1	**envelope GOOD SEASONS Italian Salad Dressing Mix**
1	**can (16 oz.) black beans, drained, rinsed**
1	**pkg. (10 oz.) frozen corn, thawed**
1	**cup chopped ripe mango**
$^1/_2$	**cup chopped red pepper**
$^1/_3$	**cup *each* chopped cilantro and chopped red onion**
$^1/_4$	**cup lime juice**

Mix all ingredients in large bowl. Refrigerate.

Serve with pita bread wedges, tortilla chips or grilled chicken. Serve in pepper halves, if desired. Makes about 5 cups.

Black Bean & Mango Salsa Salad:
Prepare recipe as directed. Add $1^1/_2$ cups cooked brown rice.

Prep Time: 10 minutes plus refrigerating

Black Bean and Mango Salsa (left) and Easy Italian Dip (right)

Salsa

THE MEXICANS MAY HAVE INVENTED IT, BUT WITH A SIMPLE CHANGE OF SEASONINGS, SALSA TAKES ON AN ITALIAN AIR—BELLISSIMO!

- 3 **cups chopped plum tomatoes**
- 1/4 **cup chopped onion**
- 1 **envelope GOOD SEASONS Italian** *or* **Garlic & Herb Salad Dressing Mix**
- 2 **Tbsp. COLAVITA Extra Virgin Olive Oil**
- 2 **Tbsp. chopped fresh basil** *or* **1 tsp. dried basil leaves**

Mix all ingredients. Refrigerate 1 hour before serving. Serve with grilled chicken, fish, vegetables or breads, or serve as a dip with tortilla chips or pita chips. Makes 3 cups.

PREP TIME: 10 MINUTES PLUS REFRIGERATING

THE GOLDEN RULE FOR TAKING FOODS SAFELY TO PICNICS OR POTLUCKS IS TO KEEP HOT FOODS HOT AND COLD FOODS COLD.

TOTING TIPS

WAIT UNTIL JUST BEFORE YOU LEAVE TO PACK BOTH TYPES. TO KEEP FOODS HOT WHILE YOU'RE ON THE ROAD, WRAP THE CONTAINER IN FOIL OR A HEAVY TOWEL AND PLACE IT IN AN INSULATED CARRIER. FOR COLD FOODS, MAKE SURE THEY'RE WELL CHILLED BEFORE YOU PLACE THEM IN A COOLER WITH ICE PACKS OR ICE.

CHEESE AND *Roll*

A BOTTLE OF WINE, A BASKET OF CRACKERS AND THIS PECAN-ENCRUSTED TWO-CHEESE SPREAD—THAT'S ALL YOU NEED FOR A PORTABLE PARTY.

- **1 pkg. (8 oz.) cream cheese, softened**
- **1¹/₂ cups shredded cheddar cheese**
- **2 Tbsp. milk**
- **2 Tbsp. *each* finely chopped green onion and finely chopped red pepper**
- **1 envelope GOOD SEASONS Garlic & Herb *or* Italian Salad Dressing Mix**
- **¹/₂ cup finely chopped pecans**

MIX cheeses and milk with electric mixer on medium speed until well blended. Add onion, red pepper and salad dressing mix; mix well. Refrigerate 30 minutes.

SHAPE cheddar cheese mixture into 8-inch roll.* Cover with pecans. Refrigerate several hours. Serve with crackers. Makes 10 to 12 servings.

*NOTE: To shape, place cheese mixture on sheet of plastic wrap; form into roll. Sprinkle with pecans, securing to top and sides of roll by pressing in with plastic wrap.

PREP TIME: 20 MINUTES PLUS REFRIGERATING

Greek

SANDWICH

To make hot Mediterranean-style sandwiches, don't fold the pita breads. Place them on a broiler pan and broil 5 to 7 inches from heat for 2 minutes or until cheese is bubbly and edges of pita breads are browned and crisp.

- 1 lb. chopped cooked chicken
- $^1/_2$ cup COLAVITA Extra Virgin Olive Oil
- $^1/_2$ cup chopped tomato
- 1 pkg. (4 oz.) ATHENOS Crumbled Feta Cheese
- 1 can ($2^1/_4$ oz.) sliced pitted ripe olives, drained
- 1 envelope GOOD SEASONS Italian *or* Zesty Italian Salad Dressing Mix
- 6 pita breads

MIX all ingredients except pita breads in medium bowl.

TOP half of each pita bread with $^1/_2$ cup chicken mixture.

FOLD pita breads. Secure with wooden toothpicks. Makes 6 servings.

PREP TIME: 10 MINUTES

S I M P L E  Chili

FOR A CHANGE OF FLAVOR PACE, TRY THIS
HEARTY CHILL-CHASER WITH GROUND PORK
OR TURKEY OR BULK ITALIAN SAUSAGE.

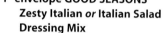

- **1 lb. ground beef**
- **1 green pepper, chopped**
- **1 envelope GOOD SEASONS**
  Zesty Italian *or* Italian Salad
  Dressing Mix
- **2 tsp. chili powder**
- **1 can (15 oz.) kidney beans, drained**
- **1 cup water**
- **1 can (8 oz.) tomato sauce**
- **1 can (4 oz.) chopped green chilies,**
  drained

BROWN meat in large skillet on medium heat.
Add green pepper, salad dressing mix and
chili powder; cook and stir until green pepper
is tender.

STIR in kidney beans, water and tomato
sauce. Bring to boil. Reduce heat to low; cover
and simmer 5 minutes, stirring occasionally.

STIR in chilies; return to boil. Serve warm with
shredded cheddar cheese, chopped onion or
sour cream, if desired. Makes about 5 cups.

PREP TIME: 15 MINUTES
COOKING TIME: 20 MINUTES

FRUITY

Chicken

This light and fresh twist on chicken salad with grapes is just the ticket for toting to a potluck, office party or picnic.

1 envelope **GOOD SEASONS Honey French** *or* **Italian Salad Dressing Mix**
3 cups **cooked orzo pasta**
2 cups **finely chopped cooked chicken**
1 cup **red** *or* **green seedless grapes**
$^1/_2$ cup **finely chopped carrots Chopped fresh parsley**

PREPARE dressing in cruet or small bowl as directed on envelope, using COLAVITA Red Wine Vinegar, water and oil.

MIX orzo, chicken, grapes and carrots in large bowl. Add $^1/_2$ cup of the dressing; toss to mix well. Cover.

REFRIGERATE salad and remaining dressing at least 2 hours. Just before serving, mix in remaining dressing. Serve on lettuce-lined plates. Sprinkle with parsley. Makes $5^1/_2$ cups.

A SALAD SANDWICH? You bet! Simply spoon Fruity Chicken Salad into pita bread halves or onto tortillas and roll up!

PREP TIME: 10 MINUTES PLUS REFRIGERATING

COOKED CHICKEN CHOICES

DON'T HAVE LEFTOVER COOKED CHICKEN TO MAKE FRUITY CHICKEN SALAD? JUST LOOK IN THE FREEZER SECTION OF YOUR SUPERMARKET FOR FROZEN COOKED CHICKEN. OR, STOP BY THE DELI COUNTER AND PURCHASE A WHOLE ROASTED BIRD. REMOVE THE MEAT FROM THE BONES AND DICE IT. USE 2 CUPS TO MAKE THE SALAD AND FREEZE THE REST FOR NEXT TIME.

THE MORE HECTIC OUR LIVES BECOME, THE MORE IMPORTANT

IT IS TO REWARD OURSELVES WITH GOOD FOOD AND

GOOD TIMES AROUND THE TABLE WITH FAMILY AND FRIENDS.

THESE MAKE-AHEAD AND LAST-MINUTE

IDEAS ARE PERFECT FOR UNEXPECTED COMPANY

ON THE WEEKEND OR FOR YOUR HUNGRY

CREW ON ANY WEEKNIGHT.

Perfect Pasta Pizza SEE RECIPE, PAGE 42

Beat
the
Clock

FOR FUN AND ADDITIONAL FLAVOR, CROWN THIS PASTA-CRUSTED PIE WITH YOUR FAVORITE PIZZA TOPPINGS! PICTURED ON PAGES 40–41.

- **8 oz. spaghetti, cooked, drained**
- **1 egg, beaten**
- **¹/₄ cup milk**
- **³/₄ lb. ground beef**
- **1 can (14 oz.) tomato sauce**
- **1 envelope GOOD SEASONS Garlic & Herb Salad Dressing Mix**
- **1 cup shredded low-moisture part-skim mozzarella cheese**

Toss spaghetti, egg and milk in large bowl. Spread evenly in greased 12-inch pizza pan.

Brown meat in medium skillet; drain. Stir in tomato sauce and salad dressing mix. Spoon over spaghetti crust. Sprinkle with cheese.

Bake at 350°F 20 to 25 minutes or until cheese is melted. Makes 4 servings.

Personalized Pasta Pizza: Prepare pizza as directed, topping meat mixture with your favorite pizza toppings, such as pepperoni, mushrooms, olives and peppers; sprinkle with cheese. Bake as directed.

Perfect Pasta Pizza with Onion: Prepare pizza as directed, adding ¹/₂ cup chopped onion to meat when browning.

PREP TIME: 15 MINUTES
BAKING TIME: 25 MINUTES

ITALIAN Meat Loaf

This flavorful meat loaf goes together in a snap—leaving you an hour to attend to other things (or just relax) as it bakes. Bake squash or potatoes alongside the meat loaf to make a meal.

1	cup dried bread crumbs
1/4	cup milk
2	lb. ground beef
1	can (8 oz.) tomato sauce *or* 1 cup ketchup, divided
3/4	cup finely chopped celery
1	envelope GOOD SEASONS Italian Salad Dressing Mix
1	egg, slightly beaten
2	Tbsp. chopped fresh parsley (optional)

SOAK bread crumbs in milk in large bowl. Add meat, 1/2 of the tomato sauce and remaining ingredients; mix thoroughly.

SHAPE meat mixture into oval loaf in shallow baking pan.

BAKE at 350°F for 1 hour. Spoon remaining tomato sauce over meat loaf. Bake an additional 20 minutes or until meat loaf is cooked through. Makes 12 servings.

TO MAKE AHEAD: Prepare meat loaf as directed, shaping meat mixture into 2 loaves. Bake 1 loaf immediately at 350°F for 50 minutes. Wrap second loaf securely; freeze. When ready to serve, bake, unwrapped, at 350°F for 1 hour 20 minutes.

Prep Time: 15 minutes
Baking Time: 1 hour 20 minutes

Cacciatore

Vary the flavor of the tomato sauce for this classic dish by choosing one of three different GOOD SEASONS Salad Dressing Mixes suggested below.

2 Tbsp. oil
4 boneless skinless chicken breast halves (about 1¼ lb.)
1 medium onion, sliced
1 medium green pepper, cut into strips
1 cup sliced mushrooms
 1 envelope GOOD SEASONS Italian, Mild Italian or Zesty Italian Salad Dressing Mix
1 can (28 oz.) crushed tomatoes with puree
Hot cooked pasta

HEAT oil in large skillet on medium-high heat. Add chicken, onion, green pepper and mushrooms; cook and stir until chicken is browned on both sides.

SPRINKLE salad dressing mix over chicken mixture. Stir in tomatoes. Bring to boil.

REDUCE heat to low; cover. Simmer 15 minutes, stirring occasionally. Serve chicken mixture over hot cooked pasta, if desired. Makes 4 servings.

PREP TIME: 10 MINUTES
COOKING TIME: 25 MINUTES

CHUNKY CHICKEN

Vegetable

GOOD SEASONS Salad Dressing Mix adds just the right spices to make this quick chicken soup taste like it was simmered all day.

- ¹/₂ **lb. boneless skinless chicken breasts, cubed**
- 1 **can (13³/₄ oz.) chicken broth**
- 1¹/₂ **cups water**
- 2 **cups assorted cut-up fresh vegetables, such as sliced carrots, broccoli flowerets and chopped red pepper, *or* 1 pkg. (10 oz.) frozen mixed vegetables, thawed**
- 1 **envelope GOOD SEASONS Italian Salad Dressing Mix**
- ¹/₂ **cup instant rice, uncooked**

COOK and stir chicken in large saucepan sprayed with no stick cooking spray until cooked through, about 8 minutes.

STIR in broth, water, vegetables and salad dressing mix. Bring to boil. Reduce heat to low; cover. Simmer 7 to 9 minutes or until vegetables are tender. (If using frozen vegetables, simmer 5 minutes.)

STIR in rice; cover. Remove from heat. Let stand 5 minutes. Makes about 5 cups.

PREP TIME: 10 MINUTES
COOKING TIME: 20 MINUTES PLUS
    STANDING

Chicken

Soak up the delicious juices from this homey chicken with hot cooked rice. Steamed green beans and a crisp salad make fine accompaniments.

- 1 large onion, sliced
- 1 broiler-fryer chicken, cut up (3 to 3^1/$_2$ lb.)
- 1 cup prepared GOOD SEASONS Italian Salad Dressing

ARRANGE onion slices in greased 13x9-inch baking dish. Place chicken over onion slices.

POUR salad dressing over chicken. Cover tightly with aluminum foil.

BAKE at 375°F for 1 hour. Remove foil. Bake an additional 15 minutes. Serve with cooked rice, if desired. Makes 6 servings.

PREP TIME: 5 MINUTES
BAKING TIME: 1 HOUR 15 MINUTES

PLAY IT SAFE

WHENEVER YOU WORK WITH RAW POULTRY OR OTHER RAW MEATS OR FISH, ALWAYS WASH YOUR HANDS THOROUGHLY BEFORE TOUCHING OTHER FOODS. ALSO, USE HOT SOAPY WATER TO WASH ALL COUNTERTOPS AFTERWARDS.

Need a quick, easy, sure-to-please snack for a hungry crowd? You can't miss with these hearty quesadillas.

2 pkg. (8 oz. *each*) shredded cheddar cheese

1 envelope GOOD SEASONS Zesty Italian *or* Italian Salad Dressing Mix

10 flour tortillas (10 inch)
Chopped tomatoes, sliced green onions, sliced ripe olives
Sour cream and salsa

Mix cheese and salad dressing mix. Place 5 of the tortillas on large cookie sheet. Spread each tortilla with ³/₄ cup cheese mixture. Top with tomatoes, onions, olives and second tortilla.

Bake at 350°F for 10 minutes. Cut each quesadilla into 12 pie-shaped wedges. Serve with sour cream and salsa. Makes 5 dozen.

Prep Time: 10 minutes
Cooking Time: 10 minutes

Take Your Pick Of
Flour Tortillas

Flour tortillas, often used as soft taco shells, come in many colors and sizes. You'll find them in the refrigerated dairy case or grocery aisle of the supermarket. You'll also find tortilla products in a variety of hues from pale pink to green to blue—often seasoned with herbs, tomatoes, spinach or sesame seeds.

GARLIC MASHED POTATOES ARE ALL THE RAGE
IN RESTAURANTS. NOW, WITH THIS EASY
RECIPE, YOU CAN MAKE THEM AT HOME.

**1 envelope GOOD SEASONS Roasted
   Garlic *or* Italian Salad Dressing Mix
4 cups prepared mashed potatoes**

STIR salad dressing mix into potatoes. Serve
immediately. Top with pat of butter, if desired.
Serve with grilled or broiled steaks, chops,
chicken or fish. Makes 4 servings.

PREP TIME: 5 MINUTES

Almost

RISOTTO

Rice-shaped orzo makes this risotto-like dish extra fast and extra easy.

1 can (13³/₄ oz.) chicken broth
1 envelope GOOD SEASONS Gourmet Parmesan Italian Salad Dressing Mix
1 cup orzo pasta, uncooked
1 jar (4¹/₂ oz.) sliced mushrooms, drained

BRING broth and salad dressing mix to boil in medium saucepan on medium-high heat.

ADD orzo. Reduce heat to low; cover. Simmer 10 minutes or until orzo is tender.

STIR in mushrooms. Serve with DI GIORNO Grated Parmesan Cheese, if desired. Makes 6 servings.

Prep Time: 5 minutes
Cooking Time: 10 minutes

Twice Baked

POTATOES

To keep these potatoes on hand, prepare as directed (do not bake) and freeze. To serve, bake frozen potatoes at 325°F 35 to 40 minutes.

- **4 medium potatoes, baked**
- **1 cup sour cream**
- **1 cup shredded cheddar cheese**
- **1/4 cup *each* milk and sliced green onions**
- **1 envelope GOOD SEASONS Gourmet Parmesan Italian *or* Cheese Garlic Salad Dressing Mix**

CUT potatoes in half lengthwise; scoop out centers leaving 1/4-inch shells.

MASH potatoes. Stir in sour cream, cheese, milk, onions and salad dressing mix. Spoon into shells. Place on cookie sheet.

BAKE at 325°F for 15 to 20 minutes. Makes 4 servings.

PREP TIME: 10 MINUTES
COOKING TIME: 20 MINUTES

SIMPLE SEASONED Breadsticks

Your favorite spaghetti and meat sauce will taste even better when you serve it with these bold-flavored breadsticks warm from the oven.

- **1 can (11 oz.) refrigerated soft breadsticks, separated, cut in half**
- **3 Tbsp. butter or margarine, melted**
- **1/2 cup (2 oz.) DI GIORNO Grated Parmesan Cheese**
- **1 envelope GOOD SEASONS Zesty Italian *or* Italian Salad Dressing Mix**

DIP breadsticks in butter. Mix cheese and salad dressing mix.

COAT breadsticks with cheese mixture. Twist and place on ungreased cookie sheet.

BAKE at 350°F for 14 to 18 minutes or until golden brown. Makes 16 breadsticks.

SIMPLE SEASONED DINNER ROLLS: Wrap coated breadsticks into circle shape. Bake as directed.

PREP TIME: 15 MINUTES
BAKING TIME: 18 MINUTES

SOMETIMES, ALL WE NEED IS AN EXCUSE—HOWEVER

SMALL—TO HAVE A PARTY. **I**T MAY BE NOTHING MORE

THAN CELEBRATING A BEAUTIFUL DAY.

WHATEVER THE OCCASION, THESE FLAVORFUL AND

EASY-TO-FIX MAIN DISHES AND ACCOMPANIMENTS

MARK IT WITH GOOD TASTE.

Impromptu Gatherings

Orange Oriental Sesame Beef Stir-Fry   SEE RECIPE, PAGE 56

Orange Oriental

SESAME BEEF STIR-FRY

For the vegetables in this super-fast and pretty recipe, try using the colorful broccoli slaw mix available in the produce section of your grocery store. Pictured on pages 54–55.

- ¹⁄₄ **cup orange juice**
- 2 **Tbsp. soy sauce**
- 1 **envelope GOOD SEASONS Oriental Sesame Salad Dressing Mix**
- ¹⁄₂ **cup oil**
- 1 **Tbsp. grated orange peel**
- 1 **clove garlic, minced**
- 1 **lb. lean boneless beef sirloin, cut into strips**
- 5 **cups assorted cut-up fresh vegetables *or* 1 pkg. (16 oz.) frozen mixed vegetables, thawed**
  Hot cooked rice

MIX juice, soy sauce, salad dressing mix, oil, peel and garlic in cruet or small bowl as directed on envelope.

HEAT 1 tablespoon of the dressing mixture in large skillet on medium heat. Add meat; cook and stir until cooked through. Add vegetables and remaining dressing mixture; cook and stir until vegetables are tender-crisp. Serve over rice. Makes 4 servings.

Prep Time: 15 minutes
Cooking Time: 10 minutes

GARLICKY

Chicken Breasts

These garlic- and cheese-encrusted chicken breasts are terrific with roasted or mashed potatoes, a crisp green salad and a dry white wine.

- **1 envelope GOOD SEASONS Roasted Garlic Salad Dressing Mix**
- **1/2 cup (2 oz.) DI GIORNO Grated Parmesan Cheese**
- **6 boneless skinless chicken breast halves (about 2 lb.)**

MIX salad dressing mix and cheese.

MOISTEN chicken in water; dip in dressing mixture. Place in shallow baking dish.

BAKE at 400°F for 20 to 25 minutes or until cooked through. Makes 6 servings.

PREP TIME: 5 MINUTES
BAKING TIME: 25 MINUTES

BREAD WITH ZING

FOR A FLAVORFUL AND CRISPY BREAD FIX-UP TO ACCOMPANY A VARIETY OF MAIN DISHES, PREPARE YOUR FAVORITE **GOOD SEASONS** SALAD DRESSING MIX AND BRUSH SOME DRESSING ON FRENCH BREAD SLICES. THEN, TOAST THE SLICES AS YOU WOULD GARLIC BREAD.

Bistro Chicken

WITH PARMESAN

BISTRO COOKING IS QUICK, CASUAL FARE. THIS DELICIOUS SALAD, WHICH CAN BE ENJOYED EITHER WARM OR CHILLED, FITS THE BILL. JUST ADD SOME CHEWY ITALIAN BREAD AND DINNER IS SERVED.

- **2 boneless skinless chicken breast halves, grilled *or* broiled, cut into $^1/_4$-inch slices**
- **2 cups cooked penne *or* rotini pasta**
- **1 cup quartered cherry tomatoes**
- **1 cup DI GIORNO Shredded Parmesan Cheese**
- **$^1/_2$ cup prepared GOOD SEASONS Gourmet Caesar *or* Italian Salad Dressing**
- **$^1/_3$ cup lightly packed fresh basil leaves, cut into strips**
- **$^1/_4$ cup *each* chopped red onion and sun-dried tomatoes, drained, chopped**

Mix all ingredients. Serve warm or chilled. Makes 4 servings.

PREP TIME: 25 MINUTES

ASIAN CHICKEN WITH Peanut Slaw

THIS LIGHT AND FRESH-TASTING DISH CAN BE MADE SUPER QUICK BY REPLACING THE SHREDDED CABBAGE AND CARROT WITH 2½ CUPS OF PRESHREDDED COLESLAW MIX.

4 **boneless skinless chicken breast halves (about 1¼ lb.)**

1 **cup prepared GOOD SEASONS Oriental Sesame Salad Dressing, divided**

2 **cups finely shredded green cabbage**

1 **medium carrot, shredded**

½ **cup roasted peanuts**

PLACE chicken on greased grill over medium-hot coals. Grill 4 to 6 minutes on each side, turning once and brushing with ½ cup of the dressing.

Toss cabbage, carrot, peanuts and remaining ½ cup dressing. Serve with chicken. Makes 4 servings.

PREP TIME: 15 MINUTES
GRILLING TIME: 12 MINUTES

Classic Greek

S A L A D

This zesty salad of red onion, cucumber, tomatoes, olives and ATHENOS Feta Cheese is similar to those served in restaurants and taverns all over the Greek Islands.

 1 pkg. (10 oz.) salad greens
 1 cup pitted ripe olives *or* Greek olives
 3 plum tomatoes, cut into wedges
 $1/2$ cup thinly sliced red onion
 $1/2$ medium cucumber, peeled, cut into wedges
 $3/4$ cup prepared GOOD SEASONS Zesty Italian *or* Italian Salad Dressing
 1 pkg. (4 oz.) ATHENOS Crumbled Feta Cheese

Toss greens, olives, tomatoes, onion and cucumber with dressing. Spoon onto serving platter.

Sprinkle with cheese. Makes 4 servings.

Classic Greek Chicken Salad: Arrange 1 lb. cooked boneless skinless chicken breasts, cut into strips, over tossed salad.

Prep Time: 10 minutes

The next time you're barbecuing, grill a few extra chicken breast

Ready-to-Use

halves to refrigerate for a speedy meal later in the

Chicken

week. You can add the cooked chicken to greens

for a main dish salad, chop it to make a

spread for sandwiches or add it to stir-fried

vegetables for a simple supper.

Save time by purchasing already cooked shrimp at your supermarket's fish counter. You'll need to buy about 12 ounces.

- **8 oz. linguine**
- **1 lb. medium shrimp, cooked, cleaned**
- **$^1/_2$ lb. pea pods**
- **1 cup prepared GOOD SEASONS Roasted Garlic Salad Dressing**

Cook linguine as directed on package, adding shrimp and pea pods during last 2 minutes of cooking time; drain.

Toss all ingredients. Serve hot or refrigerate until ready to serve. Makes 4 servings.

Marinated Garlic Shrimp with Pea Pods:
Marinate shrimp in refrigerator in additional $^1/_2$ cup prepared GOOD SEASONS Roasted Garlic Dressing 1 hour prior to preparation.

Prep Time: 5 minutes
Cooking Time: 10 minutes

Garlic Shrimp
WITH PEA PODS

ROASTED GARLIC AND Red Pepper Polenta

This hearty polenta makes a great accompaniment to grilled chicken.

- **4 cups water**
- **1 envelope GOOD SEASONS Roasted Garlic *or* Cheese Garlic Salad Dressing Mix**
- **1 cup coarse-grain yellow cornmeal**
- **1/2 cup chopped roasted red pepper**
- **1/2 cup shredded sharp cheddar cheese**

BRING water and salad dressing mix to boil in medium saucepan.

POUR cornmeal into water in a slow and steady stream, stirring continuously.

COOK on low heat 20 to 25 minutes or until polenta begins to pull away from sides of pan, stirring frequently. Add red pepper and cheese; stir until cheese is melted. Serve immediately or let cool and sauté or grill before serving. Makes 6 servings.

PREP TIME: 10 MINUTES
COOKING TIME: 30 MINUTES

CHEESY

Casserole

Serve this puffy delight for brunch or a meatless entrée. For a special touch, garnish with green onions or scallions.

10 eggs
 1 envelope GOOD SEASONS Zesty Italian *or* Italian Salad Dressing Mix
3 cups shredded Monterey Jack cheese
$^1/_2$ red *or* green pepper, chopped
$^1/_3$ cup all-purpose flour
1 tsp. baking powder
$^1/_3$ cup butter *or* margarine, melted

BEAT eggs and salad dressing mix in large bowl. Stir in cheese and red pepper.

MIX flour and baking powder. Stir flour mixture and butter into cheese mixture. Pour into greased 8-inch square baking pan.

BAKE at 375°F for 35 minutes or until golden brown. Makes 6 to 8 servings.

PREP TIME: 15 MINUTES
BAKING TIME: 35 MINUTES

GREEN ONIONS OR SCALLIONS? No matter if you call them green onions or scallions, these fresh onions with a white end and long green shoots add a deliciously mild onion flavor to foods. To use them, trim off the roots and remove any wilted, brown or damaged tops, then slice and use as much of the white end and green shoot as you like.

Italian BOWL SALAD

IN THE SUMMERTIME—WHEN TRADITIONAL PIZZA SEEMS TOO HEAVY AND HOT—THIS INNOVATIVE SALAD-AND-PIZZA-IN-ONE IS JUST THE TICKET.

1 **cup prepared GOOD SEASONS Italian *or* Gourmet Parmesan Italian Salad Dressing Mix**

1 **loaf Italian bread, cut into 16 slices, toasted *or* 1 prepared pizza crust, cut into 8 wedges**

1 **pkg. (10 oz.) salad greens**

1 **cup sliced tomatoes**

   Suggested toppings: chopped pepperoni *or* salami, shredded mozzarella cheese *or* sliced fresh mozzarella cheese balls, sliced mushrooms, chopped green pepper, pitted ripe olives, DI GIORNO Grated Parmesan Cheese, red pepper flakes, fresh oregano *or* anchovies

BRUSH about 1 tablespoon dressing on each bread slice or pizza wedge.

PLACE greens and tomatoes in bowl. Toss lightly with remaining dressing.

SPOON greens mixture over 2 bread slices or 1 pizza wedge for each serving. Top with desired toppings. Makes 8 servings.

PREP TIME: 10 MINUTES

Spinach & Orange

SALAD

This refreshing citrus and spinach salad embellished with red onions, almonds and feta cheese can take on an Italian or Asian flavor— depending on which GOOD SEASONS Salad Dressing Mix you choose.

8 cups torn spinach
1 1/2 cups fresh orange sections or 2 cans (11 oz. each) mandarin orange segments, drained
1/2 cup sliced red onion
1 pkg. (4 oz.) ATHENOS Crumbled Feta Cheese

1/3 cup toasted slivered almonds
1 cup prepared GOOD SEASONS Italian *or* Oriental Sesame Salad Dressing Mix

Toss spinach, oranges, onion, cheese and almonds in large bowl.

Pour salad dressing over spinach mixture; toss to coat. Makes 6 servings.

Prep Time: 10 minutes

Toasting gives nuts a deeper, richer flavor and helps them stay crisp

Toasting Nuts

when tossed in salads. Here's how to toast nuts: Spread them in a single layer in a shallow baking pan. Bake at 350°F for 5 to 10 minutes or until golden. Watch the nuts carefully and stir them once or twice so they don't burn.

CHEESY *Herb* Bread

This delicious recipe does garlic bread one better! Serve it with your favorite lasagna or spaghetti and meatballs.

- ½ cup (1 stick) butter or margarine, softened
- 1 envelope GOOD SEASONS Gourmet Parmesan Italian or Italian Salad Dressing Mix
- 1½ cups shredded low-moisture part-skim mozzarella cheese
- 1 loaf French bread, cut in half lengthwise

MIX butter, salad dressing mix and cheese until well blended.

SPREAD on cut surfaces of bread. Place bread on cookie sheet.

BROIL 3 to 5 inches from heat 2 to 3 minutes or until cheese mixture is bubbly. Cut into 20 slices. Makes 20 servings.

Prep Time: 10 minutes
Broiling Time: 5 minutes

Roasted Vegetable

WRAPPED SANDWICH

YOU'LL HAVE DINNER ALL WRAPPED UP WITH THESE HERB-ROASTED VEGETABLE AND CHEESE-FILLED SANDWICHES. THEY'RE NOT ONLY DELICIOUS, THEY'RE EASY, TOO.

1   envelope **GOOD SEASONS Cheese Garlic** *or* **Italian Salad Dressing Mix**
2   Tbsp. **COLAVITA Red Wine Vinegar**
2   Tbsp. **COLAVITA Extra Virgin Olive Oil**
6   cups **assorted cut-up fresh vegetables, such as peppers, broccoli, carrots, mushrooms, yellow squash, onions and zucchini**
6   **low-moisture part-skim mozzarella cheese slices**
6   **flour tortillas (6 in.)**

PREPARE salad dressing mix in cruet or small bowl as directed on envelope using red wine vinegar and olive oil. Pour over vegetables; toss lightly. Spoon into 15x10x1-inch baking pan.

BAKE at 425°F 20 minutes or until vegetables are tender, stirring occasionally.

LAYER vegetable mixture and cheese on tortillas. Place on cookie sheet.

BROIL 3 to 5 inches from heat 2 minutes or until cheese is melted. Wrap up. Makes 6 servings.

ROASTED VEGETABLE SANDWICH ROLLS: Substitute 6 sandwich rolls, split, for tortillas.

PREP TIME: 15 MINUTES
BAKING TIME: 20 MINUTES
BROILING TIME: 2 MINUTES

These delectable chicken wings are a superb addition to an early-evening appetizer buffet. If it's an after-work affair, begin the marinating in the morning so all you have to do when you get home is broil the wings and serve up the celery sticks and blue cheese dressing.

- 1 **envelope GOOD SEASONS Italian, Zesty Italian *or* Garlic & Herb Salad Dressing Mix**
- 1/2 **cup honey**
- 1/4 **cup orange juice**
- 1 **Tbsp. hot pepper sauce**
- 28 **chicken wings, separated at joints, tips discarded, *or* drumettes**

Mix salad dressing mix, honey, juice and hot pepper sauce in cruet or small bowl as directed on envelope. Reserve 1/4 cup of the dressing mixture; refrigerate.

Toss chicken with remaining dressing mixture to coat. Cover. Refrigerate 1 hour to marinate. Drain; discard dressing mixture.

Place chicken wings on rack of broiler pan. Broil 4 to 6 inches from heat 16 to 20 minutes or until chicken is cooked through, turning and brushing occasionally with reserved 1/4 cup dressing mixture. Serve with celery sticks and blue cheese dressing, if desired. Makes 28 appetizers.

Prep Time: 5 minutes plus Marinating
Broiling Time: 20 minutes

BROILING BASICS

WHEN BROILING, PLACING THE FOOD THE CORRECT DISTANCE FROM THE HEAT IS IMPORTANT. TO MAKE SURE THE FOOD IS IN THE RIGHT SPOT,

POSITION THE TOP OF THE BROILER PAN RACK SO THE SURFACE OF THE FOOD, NOT THE RACK, IS THE DISTANCE FROM THE HEAT SOURCE SPECIFIED IN THE RECIPE.

Veggie Pizza

A P P E T I Z E R

FINGER FOOD MAKES FOR EASY EATING AT INFORMAL GATHERINGS. UNLIKE ITS TRADITIONAL COUSIN, THIS CRUNCHY VEGETABLE-TOPPED PIZZA IS SERVED CHILLED—WHICH MAKES FOR CONVENIENT PRE-PARTY PREPARATION.

- **2 cans (8 oz. each) refrigerated crescent dinner rolls**
- **1 pkg. (8 oz.) cream cheese, softened**
- **1/2 cup sour cream**
- **1 envelope GOOD SEASONS Gourmet Parmesan Italian *or* Italian Salad Dressing Mix**
- **5 cups cut-up assorted fresh vegetables**
- **1 cup shredded cheddar cheese**

UNROLL dough into 4 rectangles. Press onto bottom and sides of 15x10x1-inch baking pan to form crust.

BAKE at 375°F for 11 to 13 minutes or until golden brown; cool.

MIX cream cheese, sour cream and salad dressing mix until well blended. Spread on crust. Top with remaining ingredients. Refrigerate. Cut into squares. Makes 24.

PREP TIME: 15 MINUTES PLUS
   REFRIGERATING
BAKING TIME: 13 MINUTES

Simple Celebrations

Thai Chicken and Sesame Noodles SEE RECIPE, PAGE 77

ONE OF THE DELIGHTS OF THE SPRING AND SUMMER MONTHS

IS DRIFTING BREEZILY FROM BRIDAL SHOWERS TO BIRTHDAY

PARTIES TO GRADUATIONS AND FAMILY REUNIONS.

WHEN HOSTING SUCH A CELEBRATION, HERE'S EVERYTHING

YOU NEED TO MAKE IT SIMPLE AND VERY SPECIAL.

GRILLED Pork Tenderloin

WITH CORN-PEPPER RELISH

LEAN PORK TENDERLOINS ARE GRILLED FOR A SMOKY FLAVOR AND SERVED SOUTHWEST-STYLE WITH A CHUNKY BEAN, CORN AND RED PEPPER SALSA.

2 **pork tenderloins (10 to 12 oz. each)**
1 **cup prepared GOOD SEASONS Zesty Italian *or* Italian Salad Dressing, divided**
1 **can (15 oz.) black beans, drained, rinsed**
1 **can (10 oz.) whole kernel corn, drained**
1 **red pepper, chopped**

PLACE pork on greased grill over hot coals. Grill 12 to 15 minutes or until cooked through, turning every 4 minutes and brushing with $1/2$ cup of the dressing. Cut into $1/2$-inch slices.

MIX beans, corn, red pepper and remaining dressing. Serve with pork. Makes 8 servings.

PREP TIME: 10 MINUTES
GRILLING TIME: 15 MINUTES

STORING OLIVE OIL
KEEP OLIVE OIL AT ITS PEAK BY STORING IT IN A COOL, DARK PLACE WHERE IT WILL LAST FOR UP TO A YEAR. WHEN PREPARING GOOD SEASONS SALAD DRESSING MIX WITH OLIVE OIL AND CHILLING IT, THE OLIVE OIL MAY SOLIDIFY AND THE DRESSING MAY BE TOO THICK TO POUR IMMEDIATELY. THIS WON'T AFFECT THE FLAVOR. SIMPLY LET THE DRESSING STAND AT ROOM TEMPERATURE FOR 10 TO 15 MINUTES, SHAKE OR MIX IT AND SERVE.

Thai Chicken

AND SESAME NOODLES

This sweet and spicy peanut-sauced noodle dish is as good at room temperature as it is warm, making it perfect for a buffet. Pictured on pages 74–75.

- 1 cup prepared GOOD SEASONS Oriental Sesame Salad Dressing, divided
- 1 lb. boneless skinless chicken breast halves, cut into strips
- 2 Tbsp. *each* chunky peanut butter and honey
- 1/2 tsp. crushed red pepper
- 8 oz. thin spaghetti, cooked, drained
- 3/4 cup *each* grated carrot and sliced green onions
- 1/4 cup chopped cilantro

Pour 1/3 cup of the dressing over chicken in medium bowl; toss to coat. Cover. Refrigerate 1 hour to marinate. Drain; discard dressing.

Mix remaining 2/3 cup dressing, peanut butter, honey and pepper; set aside.

Cook chicken in large skillet on medium-high heat about 8 minutes or until chicken is cooked through. Mix chicken, spaghetti, carrot, onions and cilantro in large bowl. Add peanut butter mixture; toss to coat. Garnish with cilantro sprig and carrot curls, if desired. Serve immediately. Makes 4 servings.

Prep Time: 10 minutes plus marinating
Cooking Time: 15 minutes

Perfect Pasta

For pasta that's cooked just right, test it often near the end of the cooking time suggested on the package. The pasta is done when it's tender, but still slightly firm as you bite into it. To keep the pasta from cooking any further, immediately drain it in a colander.

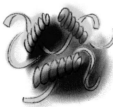

Chicken Amandine

This version of the classic is given a savory flavor boost from GOOD SEASONS Salad Dressing Mix. Try serving it over rice or a flavored pasta, such as lemon-pepper fettuccine.

1 envelope GOOD SEASONS Italian *or* Gourmet Parmesan Italian Salad Dressing Mix
$^3/_4$ cup dry white wine *or* water
$^1/_4$ cup COLAVITA Extra Virgin Olive Oil
1 lb. boneless skinless chicken breast halves
$^1/_2$ cup *each* sliced green onions and sliced almonds

MIX salad dressing mix, wine and oil in cruet or small bowl as directed on envelope.

HEAT $^1/_4$ cup of the dressing mixture in large skillet on medium heat. Add chicken; cook 8 minutes or until chicken is cooked through and browned on both sides.

ADD remaining dressing mixture, onions and almonds. Cook 4 minutes, stirring constantly. Serve over hot cooked rice or pasta. Garnish with sliced green onion, if desired. Makes 4 servings.

PREP TIME: 10 MINUTES
COOKING TIME: 12 MINUTES

CRUSTLESS Zucchini Quiche

Serve this fresh-tasting zucchini quiche at a celebratory brunch accompanied by a basket of warm muffins, biscuits or scones and an assortment of fruit juices, coffee, tea and champagne.

> 2 **cups shredded Swiss cheese, divided**
> 2 **Tbsp. flour**
> 1¼ **cups milk**
> 3 **eggs**
> 1 **envelope GOOD SEASONS Italian**
>   *or* **Mild Italian Salad Dressing Mix**
> 1 **medium zucchini, thinly sliced**

Toss 1½ cups of the cheese with flour; set aside. Beat milk, eggs and salad dressing mix with fork; stir in flour-coated cheese.

Pour into greased 9-inch pie plate. Bake at 350°F for 40 minutes.

Arrange zucchini slices in circle 1 inch from edge of quiche; sprinkle with remaining ½ cup cheese. Bake an additional 15 minutes longer or until knife inserted in center comes out clean. Makes 6 servings.

Prep Time: 5 minutes
Baking Time: 55 minutes

Shrimp Scampi

GARLIC—FROM EITHER OF TWO GREAT SALAD DRESSING MIXES—IS THE OPERATIVE INGREDIENT IN THIS DISH. BOOST ITS GREAT FLAVOR EVEN MORE BY ADDING THE FRESH GARLIC.

- 1/4 **cup** *each* **lemon juice and water**
- 1 **envelope GOOD SEASONS Garlic & Herb** *or* **Cheese Garlic Salad Dressing Mix**
- 1/4 **cup COLAVITA Extra Virgin Olive Oil, divided**
- 2 **Tbsp. chopped fresh parsley**
- 1 **tsp. minced garlic (optional)**
- 1/8 **tsp. pepper**
- 1 **small onion, chopped**
- 1 **lb. medium shrimp, cleaned**

MIX juice, water, salad dressing mix, 2 tablespoons of the olive oil, parsley, garlic and pepper in cruet or small bowl as directed on envelope. Set aside.

HEAT remaining 2 tablespoons oil in large skillet on medium heat. Add onion; cook and stir until tender but not browned. Add shrimp; cook 3 minutes or until shrimp turn pink, stirring occasionally. Stir in dressing mixture.

BRING to boil on medium heat; boil 1 minute. Serve over cooked rice or pasta. Makes 4 servings.

PREP TIME: 15 MINUTES
COOKING TIME: 10 MINUTES

SHRIMP POINTERS

TO CLEAN SHRIMP, OPEN THE SHELL OF EACH SHRIMP. WORKING FROM HEAD TO TAIL, PEEL BACK THE SHELL. TUG ON THE TAIL TO REMOVE IT. THEN, MAKE A SHALLOW CUT DOWN THE BACK OF THE SHRIMP TO EXPOSE THE VEIN. RINSE UNDER COLD RUNNING WATER TO REMOVE THE VEIN. IF NECESSARY, USE A KNIFE TO REMOVE PIECES OF VEIN AND RINSE AGAIN.

Feta Salad

To make this salad extra elegant, use ripe red pears and the flavorful mix of baby greens called Mesclun. Or, if you like, try one of the mixed greens salad combinations available at your supermarket.

- 1 fresh ripe pear, cored, thinly sliced
- 1 Tbsp. lemon juice
- 1 pkg. (10 oz.) mixed salad greens
- 1 pkg. (4 oz.) ATHENOS Crumbled Feta Cheese
- 1/2 cup coarsely chopped toasted walnuts
- 1 cup prepared GOOD SEASONS Italian *or* Mild Italian Salad Dressing

Toss pear slices with juice.

Layer greens, pear slices, cheese and walnuts in shallow salad bowl or on large serving platter.

Pour dressing over salad. Toss gently to coat. Serve immediately. Makes 6 servings.

Prep Time: 15 minutes

Bread Salad

Created by thrifty Italian cooks as a way to use day-old bread, this salad tastes its very best in summer, when the tomatoes are at their juiciest and the basil at its most prolific.

- $^1/_4$ cup COLAVITA Red Wine Vinegar
- 3 Tbsp. water
- 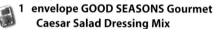 1 envelope GOOD SEASONS Gourmet Caesar Salad Dressing Mix
- $^1/_2$ cup COLAVITA Extra Virgin Olive Oil
- 4 medium red *and/or* yellow tomatoes, cut into $^1/_2$-inch chunks
- 1 medium red onion, cut into $^1/_2$-inch chunks, $^1/_2$ large cucumber, cut into $^1/_2$-inch chunks
- $^1/_3$ cup thinly sliced fresh basil
- 4 cups day-old assorted bread cubes (about 1 inch)

MIX vinegar, water, salad dressing mix and oil in cruet or small bowl as directed on envelope.

MIX remaining ingredients, except bread cubes, in large bowl. Add $^1/_2$ cup of the dressing; toss to mix well. Cover. Refrigerate.

STIR in bread cubes just before serving. Serve over mixed salad greens, if desired. Makes 8 cups or 8 to 10 servings.

PREP TIME: 15 MINUTES PLUS REFRIGERATING

TO serve Italian Tomato Bread Salad, above, in a bread bowl, CREATE A cut and discard a thin slice from the top of a large round loaf of BREAD BOWL bread. Hollow out the loaf, leaving a $^1/_2$-inch rim. Cover the bowl with plastic wrap. Cut the bread from the loaf center into cubes.

Spread in a shallow baking pan. bake at 200°F for 10 minutes.

Cool and use in the salad.

Green Bean AND MOZZARELLA CHEESE SALAD

Try making this salad with fresh Mozzarella. It's much softer than aged Mozzarella and usually comes in round balls packed in brine. If you can't find it at your supermarket, check Italian markets and specialty food stores.

2 **cups fresh green beans**
6 **plum tomatoes, sliced**
1 **pkg. (8 oz.) part-skim mozzarella cheese, cut into** $^1/_2$**-inch cubes**
$^1/_3$ **cup chopped fresh basil**
$^1/_8$ **tsp. pepper**
$^1/_3$ **cup prepared GOOD SEASONS Zesty Italian *or* Italian Salad Dressing**

Cook beans in medium saucepan in enough boiling water to cover 4 minutes or until tender-crisp. Drain. Rinse with cold water; drain.

Mix beans, tomatoes, cheese, basil and pepper in large bowl.

Add dressing; toss to coat. Serve immediately or refrigerate until ready to serve. Makes 4 servings.

Prep Time: 15 minutes
Cooking Time: 4 minutes

CHOPPING HERBS

MAKE QUICK WORK OF CHOPPING FRESH HERBS. JUST PLACE THE LEAVES IN A GLASS MEASURING CUP OR A SMALL BOWL AND CUT THEM INTO TINY PIECES WITH KITCHEN SHEARS, USING SHORT, QUICK STROKES.

GOURMET PARMESAN

Italian Pesto

Use this fragrant and easy-to-make pesto on hot cooked pasta, on grilled chicken, to flavor soups—even as a savory spread for garlic bread.

- **2 cloves garlic, minced**
- **2 cups fresh basil leaves**
- **¹/₂ cup COLAVITA Extra Virgin Olive Oil**
- **1 envelope GOOD SEASONS Gourmet Parmesan Italian *or* Italian Salad Dressing Mix**

PLACE garlic and basil in food processor or blender container; cover. Slowly drizzle oil into mixture while processor is running; process until blended.

STIR in salad dressing mix. Refrigerate until ready to serve. Toss with 1 lb. hot cooked pasta. Makes ¹/₂ cup.

PREP TIME: 10 MINUTES PLUS
REFRIGERATING

THERE ARE SEVERAL WAYS TO MINCE GARLIC QUICKLY AND EASILY.

MINCING

YOU CAN USE A GARLIC PRESS TO CRUSH THE CLOVE, SMASH IT BY

GARLIC

PLACING A FLAT SIDE OF A CHEF'S KNIFE OVER THE CLOVE AND

HITTING IT WITH THE SIDE OF YOUR FIST OR CUT A PEELED CLOVE

INTO TINY PIECES WITH A SHARP KNIFE. FOR REAL CONVENIENCE,

LOOK FOR BOTTLED MINCED GARLIC IN YOUR SUPERMARKET PRODUCE SECTION.

Bruschetta

Light and fresh, these tomato-topped bruschetta make a perfect prelude to a grilled meal. Garnish each of them with a fresh herb sprig, if desired.

- **1 loaf French bread *or* baguette, cut into 24 (1-inch) slices**
-  **1 cup prepared GOOD SEASONS Roasted Garlic *or* Garlic & Herb Salad Dressing**
- **6 green onions, chopped**
- **4 medium tomatoes, chopped**

PLACE bread slices on rack of broiler pan 3 to 5 inches from heat. Broil 2 minutes or until golden brown.

BRUSH each toast slice with 2 teaspoons dressing.

SPRINKLE with chopped vegetables. Makes 24.

Prep Time: 5 minutes
Broiling Time: 2 minutes

SPINACH

ARTICHOKE DIP

Artichoke hearts add a touch of elegance to this simple dip that's easily made ahead and chilled until serving time.

- 1 container (16 oz.) sour cream
- 1 can (14 oz.) artichoke hearts, drained, chopped
- 1 pkg. (10 oz.) frozen chopped spinach, thawed, well drained
- 1 envelope GOOD SEASONS Italian Salad Dressing Mix

- $^1/_2$ cup chopped red pepper (optional)
- $^1/_4$ cup chopped green onions

Mix all ingredients. Refrigerate.

Serve with assorted cut-up vegetables or pita chips. Makes 4 cups.

Prep Time: 10 minutes plus refrigerating

HOT GARLIC Artichoke Dip

Vegetable dippers and sturdy chips are tasty ways to scoop up this velvety artichoke-and-Parmesan cheese combination.

- 1 can (14 oz.) artichoke hearts, drained, chopped
- 1 cup mayonnaise
- 1 cup (4 oz.) DI GIORNO Grated Parmesan Cheese
- 1 envelope GOOD SEASONS Roasted Garlic *or* Garlic & Herb Salad Dressing Mix

- 2 Tbsp. *each* sliced green onion and chopped tomato

Mix all ingredients, except onion and tomato, until blended.

Spoon into 9-inch pie plate.

Bake at 350°F for 20 to 25 minutes or until lightly browned. Sprinkle with onion and tomato. Makes 2 cups.

Prep Time: 10 minutes
Baking Time: 25 minutes

GOOD SEASONS®
MAKES A GREAT MARINADE
FOR MEATS, FISH AND VEGETABLES!

Prepare desired marinade (see recipes below) or prepare a favorite GOOD SEASONS Salad Dressing Mix according to envelope directions. Pour dressing over meat or vegetables and marinate according to chart below. For food safety reasons, do not marinate meat and vegetables together, and discard marinade after use.

Meat or Vegetable	Amount to Marinate	Time to Marinate (in the refrigerator)
Beef	1 lb.	4 hours to overnight
Chicken	1$^1/_2$ lb.	1 hour to overnight
Fish	1 lb.	30 minutes to 1 hour
Vegetables	1$^1/_2$ lb.	30 minutes to 1 hour

▪ **BASIC MARINADE:** Mix 1 envelope any flavor GOOD SEASONS Salad Dressing Mix in cruet or small bowl as directed on envelope.

▪ **CITRUS MARINADE:** Mix 1 envelope GOOD SEASONS Italian Salad Dressing Mix, $^1/_3$ cup oil and $^1/_3$ cup orange juice in cruet or small bowl as directed on envelope.

▪ **ITALIAN MARINADE:** Mix 1 envelope GOOD SEASONS Italian *or* Zesty Italian Salad Dressing Mix, $^1/_3$ cup COLAVITA Extra Virgin Olive Oil, $^1/_3$ cup dry white wine and 2 Tbsp. lemon juice in cruet or small bowl as directed on envelope.

▪ **TERIYAKI MARINADE:** Mix 1 envelope GOOD SEASONS Italian Salad Dressing Mix, $^1/_4$ cup HEINZ Apple Cider Vinegar, $^1/_4$ cup oil, $^1/_4$ cup soy sauce and 2 Tbsp. honey in cruet or small bowl as directed on envelope.

Pairing the right wine with the right food heightens and enhances the flavors of both, which makes for a thoroughly satisfying dining experience. But what wine to choose? The good news these days is that picking the right wine to go with what you are serving is not nearly as daunting as it used to be. Most wine experts have thrown out the rules about serving white wine with poultry, fish and seafood, and red wine with red meats—insisting instead that your own tastes and instincts should take precedence. The key is to match the wine to the distinctive flavors of the foods you're serving. Here are some wine basics to get you started:

BUYING WINE

Most wines are available in 750 ml bottles; some—particularly champagne—also come in magnums (1.5 L). One 750 ml bottle provides about five 5-ounce servings; a magnum will generally serve twice as many.

WINE TYPES

Wines sipped with appetizers before dinner, including dry sherry and vermouth, are called apéritifs. Dessert wines, such as muscat, cream sherry, Marsala and ruby port, are served with sweets or after a meal. Sparkling wines such as French champagne and Italian spumante can be served before, during or after a meal.

Table or dinner wines include white, red, and blush or rosé wines. White wines are generally light in body and flavor and can be dry and tart or sweet and fragrant. Red wines run the color spectrum from purple-red, brick-red or ruby-red. They are dry and rich, sometimes with a tart or astringent quality. Blush or rosé wines can be either dry or sweet. Table wines can also be served with appetizers.

SERVING WINE

Most wines don't need to "breathe" and they don't need decanting. Drinking wine at the ideal temperature, however, is essential to enjoying its qualities at their best. Red table wines should be served at cool room temperature (60° to 65° F); white wines cool, but not ice-cold (about 50° F); and blush or rosé wines, as well as sparkling wines, well-chilled (40° to 50° F).

You don't need special glasses for white and red wines, either. One good, all-purpose wine glass works just fine—either a 7- or 8-inch tulip or balloon-shaped glass. Sparkling wines, though, do best in flutes to keep their bubbles from escaping from a large surface area.

STORING WINE

For long-term storage, keep wine in a cool, well-ventilated space. The ideal temperature for storage is 55° to 60° F. Ten degrees higher or lower is fine, too. Store uncorked wine bottles on their sides so the corks don't dry out and let in air. Metal- or plastic-capped bottles can be stored upright.

WINE GUIDE

Type	Flavor	Suggested Foods
WHITE TABLE WINES		
Chablis (shah-BLEE)	Dry; fresh & fruity	Oysters, light chicken dishes
Chardonnay (shahr-don-AY)	Dry; medium- to full-bodied	Seafood, pork, tuna, chicken
Chenin Blanc (SHEN-ihn BLAHNK)	Dry to semisweet; light-bodied	Brie, green grapes, seafood
Gewürztraminer (guh-VERT-strah-mee-nuhr)	Dry to semisweet; light-bodied; spicy	Spicy foods, gumbo
Pinot Blanc (PEE-noh BLAHNK)	Dry; slightly fruity; light-bodied	Seafood
Pinot Grigio (PEE-noh GREE-jo)	Dry; light-bodied	Seafood, fish, poultry, antipasto
White Riesling (REEZ-ling)	Dry to sweet; light-bodied	Pears; blue cheese; light chicken dishes
Sauvignon Blanc (soh-veen-YOHN BLAHNK)	Dry & crisp; light- to medium-bodied	Goat cheese, seafood
Soave (SWAH-vay)	Dry; light-bodied	Seafood, fish, poultry, antipasto
RED TABLE WINES		
Bardolino (bahr-dihl-EE-noh)	Dry; light-bodied	Turkey, fish, veal, risotto, pizza
Beaujolais Nouveau (boh-zhoh-LAY noo-VOH)	Young & fruity; light-bodied	Chicken, steak
Burgundy	Medium- to heavy-bodied	Beef stew, duck
Bordeaux (bohr-DOH)	Light & fresh to strong & hard-edged	Lamb, hard cheeses
Cabernet Sauvignon (kah-buhr-NAY soh-veen-YOHN)	Rich & dry; medium- to full-bodied	Game dishes, roast beef
Chianti (kee-AHN-tee)	Dry & fruity; medium-bodied	Lamb or beef
Merlot (mehr-LOH)	Dry; light- to full-bodied	Lamb, veal, strong cheeses, steak, lasagna
Pinot Noir (PEE-noh NWAHR)	Smooth; light-bodied	Salmon, strong cheeses
Shiraz (also called Syrah)	Spicy & smooth; rich; medium- to strong-bodied	Spicy foods, grilled poultry, grilled meats
Zinfandel (ZIHN-fuhn-dehl)	Light- to strong-bodied	Paté, steak, veal, pizza
BLUSH OR ROSÉ WINE		
Grenache (gruh-NAHSH)	Dry to semisweet	Light main courses
White Zinfandel (ZIHN-fuhn-dehl)	Slightly sweet	Pizza, nachos, fried chicken
SPARKLING WINES		
Champagne	Very dry to sweet	Appetizers
Spumante (spoo-MAHN-tay)	Sweet & fruity	Desserts

Index

CREDITS
GOOD SEASONS Project Coordinators: Sally Behrhorst, Stephanie Lo, Lisa Pollock, Anurag Wadehra
GOOD SEASONS Recipe Development and Testing: Kristie Roehr
Produced by: Meredith Custom Publishing

METRIC COOKING HINTS

By making a few conversions, cooks in Australia, Canada, and the United Kingdom can use the recipes in *GOOD SEASONS® Casual Entertaining* with confidence. The charts on this page provide a guide for converting measurements from the U.S. customary system, which is used throughout this book, to the imperial and metric systems. There also is a conversion table for oven temperatures to accommodate the differences in oven calibrations.

Product Differences: Most of the ingredients called for in the recipes in this book are available in English-speaking countries. However, some are known by different names. Here are some common American ingredients and their possible counterparts:

- Sugar is granulated or castor sugar.
- Powdered sugar is icing sugar.
- All-purpose flour is plain household flour or white flour. When self-rising flour is used in place of all-purpose flour in a recipe that calls for leavening, omit the leavening agent (baking soda or baking powder) and salt.
- Light-colored corn syrup is golden syrup.
- Cornstarch is cornflour.
- Baking soda is bicarbonate of soda.
- Vanilla is vanilla essence.
- Green, red or yellow sweet peppers are capsicums.
- Golden raisins are sultanas.

Volume and Weight: Americans traditionally use cup measures for liquid and solid ingredients. The chart, above right, shows the approximate imperial and metric equivalents. If you are accustomed to weighing solid ingredients, the following approximate equivalents will be helpful.

- 1 cup butter, castor sugar, or rice = 8 ounces = about 250 grams
- 1 cup flour = 4 ounces = about 125 grams
- 1 cup icing sugar = 5 ounces = about 150 grams

Spoon measures are used for smaller amounts of ingredients. Although the size of the tablespoon varies slightly in different countries, for practical purposes and for recipes in this book, a straight substitution is all that's necessary.

Measurements made using cups or spoons always should be level unless stated otherwise.

EQUIVALENTS: U.S. = AUSTRALIA/U.K.

$^1/_8$ teaspoon = 0.5 ml
$^1/_4$ teaspoon = 1 ml
$^1/_2$ teaspoon = 2 ml
1 teaspoon = 5 ml
1 tablespoon = 1 tablespoon
$^1/_4$ cup = 2 tablespoons = 2 fluid ounces = 60 ml
$^1/_3$ cup = $^1/_4$ cup = 3 fluid ounces = 90 ml
$^1/_2$ cup = $^1/_3$ cup = 4 fluid ounces = 120 ml

$^2/_3$ cup = $^1/_2$ cup = 5 fluid ounces = 150 ml
$^3/_4$ cup = $^2/_3$ cup = 6 fluid ounces = 180 ml
1 cup = $^3/_4$ cup = 8 fluid ounces = 240 ml
$1^1/_4$ cups = 1 cup
2 cups = 1 pint
1 quart = 1 litre
$^1/_2$ inch = 1.27 cm
1 inch = 2.54 cm

BAKING PAN SIZES

American	Metric
8x1$^1/_2$-inch round baking pan	20x4-centimetre cake tin
9x1$^1/_2$-inch round baking pan	23x3.5-centimetre cake tin
11x7x1$^1/_2$-inch baking pan	28x18x4-centimetre baking tin
13x9x2-inch baking pan	30x20x3-centimetre baking tin
2-quart rectangular baking dish	30x20x3-centimetre baking tin
15x10x1-inch baking pan	30x25x2-centimetre baking tin (Swiss roll tin)
9-inch pie plate	22x4- or 23x4-centimetre pie plate
7- or 8-inch springform pan	18- or 20-centimetre springform or loose-bottom cake tin
9x5x3-inch loaf pan	23x13x7-centimetre or 2-pound narrow loaf tin or paté tin
1$^1/_2$-quart casserole	1.5-litre casserole
2-quart casserole	2-litre casserole

OVEN TEMPERATURE EQUIVALENTS

Fahrenheit Setting	Celsius Setting*	Gas Setting
300°F	150°C	Gas Mark 2 (slow)
325°F	160°C	Gas Mark 3 (moderately slow)
350°F	180°C	Gas Mark 4 (moderate)
375°F	190°C	Gas Mark 5 (moderately hot)
400°F	200°C	Gas Mark 6 (hot)
425°F	220°C	Gas Mark 7
450°F	230°C	Gas Mark 8 (very hot)
Broil		Grill

* Electric and gas ovens may be calibrated using Celsius. However, for an electric oven, increase the Celsius setting 10 to 20 degrees when cooking above 160°C. For convection or forced-air ovens (gas or electric), lower the temperature setting 10°C when cooking at all heat levels.